and her garden

Shoo Rayner

Oxford University Press

Oxford University Press, Walton Street, Oxford OX2 6DP

Oxford   New York
Athens   Auckland   Bangkok   Bombay
Calcutta   Cape Town   Dar es Salaam   Delhi
Florence   Hong Kong   Istanbul   Karachi
Kuala Lumpur   Madras   Madrid   Melbourne
Mexico City   Nairobi   Paris   Singapore
Taipei   Tokyo   Toronto

and associated companies in
Berlin   Ibadan

Oxford is a trade mark of Oxford University Press

ISBN 0 19 916172 0

The Lydia books are:

Lydia and her garden
Lydia and the letters
Lydia and the present
Lydia and her cat
Lydia at the shops
Lydia and the ducks

Lydia book pack: ISBN 0 19 916171 2

It was raining.
Lydia was sad.

She wanted to play outside.

'We can make a garden inside,' said Mum.

She put some blotting paper in a dish.

She sprinkled on some seeds and water.

Lydia made it look like a garden.

She watered the garden every day.

The cress seeds grew and grew.

Soon the cress was ready to eat.

Mum cut some cress.
'I'm hungry', said Lydia.

Mum made cheese and cress sandwiches.

Lydia took a big bite.

'Oh! I don't like cress!' said Lydia.